The Sales Agent Survival Guide

THINGS EVERY SALESPERSON SHOULD KNOW
BUT NOBODY TELLS THEM

CHARLES LEWIS

Copyright © 2023 Charles Lewis

All rights reserved.

ISBN: 9798375102153

DEDICATION

This book is dedicated to my son, as he embarks on his sales journey

CONTENTS

1	The Sales Training Gap	1
2	The Bridge	3
3	Your Superpower	9
4	Like + Trust = Buy	13
5	Your Most Valuable Asset	21
6	Second Most Valuable Asset	27
7	The Sales Process	35
8	Awareness of Need	37
9	Identify Options	43
10	Select Best Value	51
11	Finalize Purchase	61
12	Beyond Positive Thinking	69
13	Tenacity	75
14	Spending the Money	79

1 - THE SALES TRAINING GAP

When a salesperson starts a new job, the training usually covers the product or services that will be sold, a little about the company, and all the internal systems and process which will be used to capture customer information, create quotes, and finalize transactions. There will also be detailed instructions on what the new salespeople will be expected to do, but rarely will these new salespeople be taught effective ways to engage with and persuade customers.

Even though this is exactly what they're hired to do, the thinking is that since there is a lot of information thrown at them in the beginning, the number one priority is just to get them up and running. This makes sense, but how is that any different than giving a solider a gun with no instructions on how to operate it? Just send them out into the field and hopefully they'll figure it out.

That is precisely what most sales training is like. A new salesperson will be told they are expected to talk to customers, create quotes, close transactions, and follow up if customers don't buy, but very rarely will the anybody talk about things like:

- What are some ways to modify a sales presentation to match a customer's personality type, so the information being presented is more persuasive?
- What are some ways to ask questions so that your

customers reveal the true reasons they have not bought your product or service?
- What are your customers really looking for in the different stages of the sales process?

This book intends to fill in that gap. Anybody can "talk" to customers, but it takes skills to be an effective salesperson. Some of those skills can be learned by trial-and-error, over a long period of time, and talking to enough customers. The problem with this approach is you MIGHT learn to do it right AFTER doing it wrong many, many times. The name does have the word "error" in it.

If a salesperson is making mistakes, that means they've probably lost some sales, and lost sales means lost income. How much of your income are you willing to put at risk, hoping you can figure this out on your own?

The chapters in this book are intentionally brief, so the information can be absorbed quickly and implemented immediately. Some salespeople have told me they keep this book within reach during the workday. Downtime and short breaks can provide enough time to digest a page or two and then quickly try it out with customers.

Which brings up the importance of practice. Consider what it takes for baseball player to get to the Major League. It may have only taken a few minutes in the beginning to show that player the correct way to swing a bat, but it required years of practice to perfect that swing. If that player was ever in a hitting slump, the first thing they will do is go back to the basics and focus on the fundamentals.

I encourage you to think of this book as your fundamentals, but you don't have to wait until you're in a slump to come back to it. No matter how you might use this book, if it helps you increase your production, I would love to hear about it.

2 - THE BRIDGE

Salespeople are the bridge between the companies and individuals who produce products or offer services and the customers who buy them. In the case of a sole proprietor, the owner might function as both the salesperson and the manufacturer or service provider.

The sales mindset is often incorporated into the design and development of products and services. An example would be a customer survey which attempts to uncover likes/dislikes, preferences, and wants/needs. This information can be used to modify products or service offerings to make them more appealing to the target market.

There is no aspect of our lives that is not touched by sales. We use sales skills to win the attention of our love interest, and we use them when we interview for jobs. We even use sales skills when we persuade our friends or family to go to the restaurant we like instead of the one they want to go to.

We are also on the receiving end of a continual barrage of sales messages, and not just ones trying to sell us something. Some of these sales messages have the power to alter the direction of our lives. They can influence our educational paths and career choices. They can shape our lifestyle preferences, political affiliations, and religious practices.

For the purpose of this book, we will limit our discussion

to sales as it relates to commerce – when a product or a service is offered for sale and a customer pays money to buy it. Whether that customer is an individual or a business, three things must happen before a sale will take place.
- The product or service must satisfy a need or solve a problem.
- The customer must be educated on the benefits of the product or service.
- The perceived use-value of the product or service must be greater than the cost to buy it.

When these three things happen, a sales transaction will occur. There is no maybe about it. When value exceeds cost, a sale happens EVERY SINGLE TIME.

Customers will never seek out a product or service if they don't know about it, and once customers become aware of a product or service, they'll never buy it unless:
- They understand how it can benefit them, and
- They BELIEVE it will benefit them.

Salespeople educate customers about the products or services being offered so that the customer can understand the features and benefits. Salespeople influence and persuade customers to believe that the use-value of the product or service is more valuable than the purchase price. Salespeople create industries, drive economies, and create fortunes.

You don't believe that? Well, let me ask you this – how long have Americans been drinking orange juice at breakfast?

In the early 1900's, oranges were shipped from Florida and California to grocery stores across the United States. Back then, the fruit was either eaten fresh or juiced in the home. In 1909, the orange growers met to discuss a huge problem they all faced. They had grown more oranges than they could sell. In that meeting, those growers decided that instead of throwing away all those unsold oranges, they would juice them.

This created a whole new problem for them because now they had to figure out how to sell the juice.

They launched an aggressive advertising campaign which promoted the benefits of the Vitamin C found in orange juice. Eventually scientists perfected the process for creating concentrate and when we fast forward to today, one out of every five Americans drink orange juice every single morning.

So instead of throwing away those unsold oranges or decreasing the size of their groves to mirror the demand, those salespeople created a $29.7 billion dollar industry.

There is unlimited income available in the sales profession. A salesperson can make more money than any rock star, rap star, professional athlete, or movie star.

Of course, not every sales position offers an unlimited income potential. In fact, most sales positions were created by the original salesperson who started the company. That original salesperson created so much customer demand that they needed help to take all the orders.

The ones who create the demand have the highest income potential, while the ones performing the tasks associated with taking and filling the orders will make the least.

Here's a question for you. If someone fully understood that by choosing a sales career, it would be possible to make as much money as that person was capable of imagining, why don't more people embrace sales?

A major reason is there are negative connotations associated with sales. What are some of the first things that come to mind when you think about salespeople? They're pushy. They're arrogant. They're untrustworthy. They don't care about me because they're only interested in making the sale.

Can you think of any others?

Where do all these negative ideas from?

My guess is they stem from our desire to be independent. To make our own choices. How much more likely are you to do something if you thought of it, rather than if someone else told you to do it?

There's something about our nature that when it's time to spend money, even if someone presents us with the perfect solution – if they tell us to do it, there is resistance. But once we accept that it's the right thing to do, we do it because WE decided to do it. Not because THEY told us to.

Have you ever wanted to buy something, but weren't sure how to differentiate between all the options available? It could be anything. A car. A major electronics purchase like a TV or a computer. Or how about some kind of professional service? An attorney. A doctor. An accountant. A real estate agent.

If they were all the same, it would simply be a matter of choosing the cheapest one.

We like to think it's always about the price, but that is NEVER the case. There is no product category or service offering where the available options are identical. The problem is when we begin comparing all the features and benefits, it gets complicated very quickly.

A Toyota Corolla and a Honda Civic are both compact cars with good fuel efficiency. If you wanted to buy a car, how could you differentiate between the two and decide which one was best?

Of course, this assumes you've already narrowed the list of all vehicles to the compact car category and that you've narrowed the list of all compact models to only these two. You would have gone through a process to get to these two and will go through another one to decide between them.

Everyone from the manufacturer to the dealership, from

the salesperson to your family and friends, from the strangers who wrote online reviews to the advertising agency who created the brochures, websites, and TV commercials, they've all provided information you've absorbed (whether consciously or not.) All that information, even if some of it conflicts, will be mixed together, processed and will ultimately shape your purchase decision.

Every single one of these information sources is trying to influence your decision. They're trying to persuade you that their version of the facts is the right one for you. They are all salespeople, and nearly all of them will make money if you buy what they're selling.

3 - YOUR SUPERPOWER

Megan is a new real estate agent who thinks she can succeed by using "unconventional" methods. In other words, she doesn't want to come across as a salesperson. She doesn't want to be pushy. She is good with people and has a lot of friends, so she thinks she can rely on her personality and social skills.

My question is how is any of that NOT sales?

Let's consider an example. The telemarketer who interrupts you and tries to convince you to change your cable provider is performing a lead generation activity called cold calling. The strategy is to call someone you don't know to uncover a sales opportunity. Depending on the product or service being offered, it might even be possible to close the sale during that initial phone call.

If your job was to make these phone calls, your compensation would be tied to how many sales you could create out of "thin air." You would be calling people you don't know, and they might have no pre-existing knowledge about your product or service, but during the course of a five-to-ten-minute phone call, you would convince them to buy what you're selling.

You would be trained on things like establishing rapport and overcoming objections. Everything you did would be measured and compared to everyone else in the call center. You probably would be reading from a script when you made the calls. That script would direct you to say one thing if the customer said "yes" and another thing if they said "no."

You would be working in a noisy environment and be under constant pressure to produce results. Your manager would listen to your calls and coach you to say things slightly differently than what seemed natural. Your job might even be in jeopardy if you weren't able to close a high enough percentage of the calls you made.

Don't you think anyone performing a job like that would learn to be a little pushy? Not to mention that the very nature of making an unsolicited cold call is pushy. You're interrupting someone to talk about something they weren't even thinking about before they answered their phone.

As you're delivering your sales presentation, whatever reason the customer might come up with not to buy, you would counter with one of the thousands of objection handlers you have been taught. These are designed to convince the customer that what they're thinking is wrong and what you're telling them is right.

If this single sales activity is your definition of being a salesperson, then maybe we need to clarify some parts of the sales process.

The goal of the sales process is to produce sales and lead generation is a vital part of this process. A simple definition for lead generation is finding new sales opportunities, but this does not always mean finding customers with an immediate need for the product or service you are selling.

Some sales processes take longer than others. For the

most part, the more expensive the product or service, the longer the sales process will be. For example, you can expect the sales process for buying a house to be longer than the sales process for buying a new pair of athletic shoes.

Even though the length of time to complete the sales process for these two examples would be different, the steps would identical.

1. Awareness of need.
2. Identify options.
3. Select best value.
4. Finalize purchase.

Someone who buys a new pair of athletic shoes might go through all four of these steps in one day at one store. Theoretically, it would be possible to move that quickly through the first three steps when purchasing a house, but most people spend a considerable amount of time at step one before moving forward.

So, depending on the length of the sales process for your product or service, lead generation could be as broad as finding someone who MIGHT have a need for your product or service at some point in the future.

There are thousands of ways to generate leads and cold calling is only one of them. Also remember that cold calling may not be an effective lead generation strategy for all products and services. Divorce attorneys and heart surgeons would be a couple of examples.

Regardless of the method used to generate leads, the goal of the sales process is to produce sales. The telemarketer's strategy is to cold call a prospect, pitch the features and benefits of the product or service, and close the sale – all in the same conversation. Let's consider an alternate approach.

Let's say Megan (the new real estate agent at the start of this chapter) calls her best friend, named Susan. They talk for about fifteen minutes about everything that's been going on. Somewhere after catching up on all the kids' sporting activities and school awards, Megan mentions that she wasn't happy with her previous cable provider. She boasts about how much cheaper her new provider is and how many more features she has with her new plan.

Susan becomes curious about how she can get the same kind of deal. If Megan was able to take the order, how likely would it be that Susan would convert to the new provider right there on the spot? In fact, how successful do you think Megan would be in converting all her friends to the new provider if she used this same approach?

Megan would likely be ultra-successful converting her friends to the new provider, primarily because she has one very important thing the telemarketer doesn't.

Because of their existing relationship, Megan has established a level of trust with Susan. If Megan tells Susan something, Susan will accept it as true without any kind of verification or fact checking.

Depending on the level of trust Megan has with Susan, Megan could even lie to her, and Susan would believe it – based on Megan's previous track record of providing accurate information.

Disclaimer: I am in no way suggesting that it is ever necessary to abuse trust and/or lie for financial gain. In fact, a single instance of breach of trust can not only sour a relationship but can wipe away decades worth of work building credibility.

4 - LIKE + TRUST = BUY

"If people like, you, they will listen to you, but if they trust you, they will buy from you."

— Zig Zigler

Everyone can think of at least one example of something that was learned in childhood, believed for years, but turned out to be untrue. Regardless of where the original information came from – parents, older siblings, teacher, minister – the primary reason it was originally accepted as true was because it came from a trusted source.

Believing information from a trusted source is something that happens all the time, (whether we're aware of it or not.) In many cases, this kind of trust is built over time. A friend is a great example. In the beginning, you might not even know if you like the person. Over time, as you share experiences together, you grow to trust your friend.

In other cases, trust is given to a person who holds a

position of authority, such as a boss. You might not trust everything your boss says concerning all topics – politics, religion, lifestyle, for example. But within the confines of company policy and what you need to do to get promoted, you likely will believe whatever your boss tells you without any kind of verification or fact checking.

In the case of a sales transaction, very rarely will you have a pre-existing relationship with the salesperson. Rest assured though, that salesperson has gone to great lengths to prepare for your initial meeting.

Salespeople want to present themselves as someone you can easily like and trust. Ideally, they want you to feel that way about them almost immediately after meeting them.

This includes things like the clothes they wear and the hair style they choose. They will look you in the eyes when they talk to you. They are also very aware of how they speak and what they talk about.

They've learned details about the product or service they're selling so they can speak with authority concerning the features and benefits. They probably also know a lot about the competitors. Very rarely will salespeople say anything negative about the competition, but they will give you a long list of reasons why their product or service is superior.

The type of image salespeople attempt to project will vary depending on the type of product or service being sold and the type of customer who typically buys it. By design, you will feel very different at your initial meeting in an attorney's office than you will in the Apple store.

Another part of this is to project the type of image the customer is expecting. This can work either way. A customer interested in buying Apple products might expect an informal, modern atmosphere. If the sales meeting for an Apple product demonstration was held in an attorney's office, with dark wood paneling on the walls, a huge oak desk and shelves full of law books, there would be a disconnect between what was expected and the image being projected.

If the customer was a single person looking to upgrade their phone, the more formal atmosphere might work against the salesperson. But what if the customer was the purchasing agent for a major company who was interested in buying phones for the entire sales department?

Everything about the environment where the sales presentation takes place, and everything about the salesperson who gives the presentation, will either help or hurt in establishing and building trust with the customer.

That customer will never tell you whether or not they trust you, but if you don't earn their trust, they'll never buy your product or service — no matter how good the deal might be.

Let's consider an example. Let's say you've decided you want to buy a Rolex watch. You walk into a jewelry store, and see several glass display cases stocked with jewelry, diamonds, and watches. The store is clean and well lit. There is a security guard positioned near the entrance and the salesperson who greets you is dressed in an expensive designer suit.

After you inquire about Rolex watches, the salesperson gestures to the ones they have available. You view them through the glass top of the display case and then point to one you like. The salesperson unlocks the case, gently removes the watch, and then places it on a felt pad on the top of the display case.

The salesperson speaks with authority about the features and benefits of the Rolex watch you've selected. He might tell you about the precision of the movement, the quality of the band, and the value of encrusted jewels.

He then helps you place the watch on your wrist and asks, "How does that feel?"

This is important because no one buys a high-end item like a Rolex watch because of what it does. If it was only about functionality, you would buy a twenty-dollar watch at Walmart or use the clock on your phone.

The reason someone buys a Rolex is because they CAN buy a Rolex. Just the thought of having a twenty-thousand-dollar piece of jewelry around your wrist will make you feel a certain way.

That salesperson knows that if he can amplify what you're feeling when you're wearing that Rolex, there is a much higher likelihood you will buy it.

Let's back up and start over. Instead of walking into that jewelry store, you decide to meet a seller you found online in the parking lot outside Home Depot. As you get out of your car, a man walks over to greet you. His hair is unkempt, and he has a scraggly beard. He's wearing shorts and a faded Guns-n-Roses T-shirt.

He opens the liftgate of his rundown 2001 Kia Sorento. You notice it's packed full of various items. You can see what looks like an old desk behind a bunch of boxes. There are a couple of books and vinyl albums stacked near the front and behind them are two large trash bags, stuffed with what might be clothes.

The man reaches behind one of those large stuffed trash bags to retrieve a crumpled brown grocery sack. He reaches inside the sack and pulls out a Rolex watch. He hands it to you and says, "These sell for nearly twenty grand in the store, but I'll sell it to you for five if you have cash. What do you think?"

There are many things about this environment, the salesperson and the sales presentation that don't align with the type of product being offered for sale. Your initial thoughts would probably be something skeptical like, "How can I verify this is an authentic Rolex," or "How do I know this isn't stolen?"

In other words, there would be no trust established and you would need some way to verify what this salesperson was telling you.

Let's say he showed you a receipt and claimed his father had purchased the watch. He then showed you a death certificate and said he was liquidating his father's belongings and nobody else in the family wanted the watch. Even with all this backup documentation, you might still be skeptical and pass on the seventy-five-percent discount.

In the jewelry store, you believed everything the salesperson told you and were probably willing to pay full retail price for the watch. In the Home Depot parking lot though, even when offered an incredible savings, you would likely choose not to buy because you didn't TRUST the salesperson.

*****

This might be a good time to pause and ask yourself what are some things that might need to change in your sales environment and/or your sales presentation that would make it easier for customers to trust you?

Remember, customers will never tell you they don't trust you. They will only tell you "no" and not buy from you. Your ability to get a "yes" and close more sales might be as simple as making yourself appear more trustworthy.

*****

5 - YOUR MOST VALUABLE ASSET

Without spending a lot of time overthinking it, how would you answer the following questions:
- Can anyone be a salesperson?
- Can anyone succeed as a salesperson?
- Does everyone succeed as a salesperson?

The correct answers are Y,Y,N, so it follows that we all have the capacity to succeed in sales, but for some reason not everyone does. Would you like to hear a theory of why that is?

Let's start by defining the critical requirement to both function as a salesperson and succeed as a salesperson. Your most valuable asset as a salesperson is your ability to communicate with other people.

You won't get very far in sales (or life, for that matter) if you think you can force people to do what you want them to do. This is true even in the military, where giving and obeying orders is the foundation of the chain of command. The only reason that system works is because the ones receiving the orders fear the consequences of not obeying.

Fear is not the ideal motivator. In fact, anyone who has

held a position of rank in the military will tell you that one of the highest priorities when taking a new command is to gain the trust and respect of subordinates. A good leader inspires subordinates to WANT to do what they're told.

This brings us back to communication, which is the most valuable asset of any salesperson.

- To be a salesperson, you must be able to communicate with your customers.
- To succeed as a salesperson, you must learn to EFFECTIVELY communicate with your customers.
- Those who don't succeed as salespeople are unwilling to learn effective ways to communicate with customers.

Let's start by trying to define what effective communication is. Within the confines of the sales process, effective communication means that everything the salesperson says and does is designed to lead customers to a state where they choose to buy the product or service being offered.

We all like to think that logic plays a huge role in the purchase decision, but here's the reality – Emotion is what causes us to act, and logic is how we justify our decision.

You might want to read that again because it's critical that you understand it. You might also take a minute to recall a couple of times when you decided to buy something. As you reflect on those experiences now, how big of a role did emotion play in making your decision?

You may have spent months "doing your research." You may have created spreadsheets comparing features and benefits. You may have talked to hundreds of people to get their insights and opinion. All that led to the point where you FELT like you had found the right product or service.

You could visualize yourself owning it. You WANTED to own it. You willingly gave the salesperson your money so you could own it. After you bought it, you used all the information you gathered during your "research" stage to assure yourself that you had made the right decision.

To succeed in sales, all you need to do to is learn how to move customers to the state where they FEEL like your product or service is the right decision for them. Unfortunately, it's not possible to learn a magic phrase that will cause customers to feel a certain way, but it is possible to lead your conversations, so your customer begins to talk about things that makes him/her feel a certain way.

To understand how this works, it's important to realize that communication is a two-way exchange. After you are done talking, LISTEN to what your customer says. Ask questions and LISTEN some more.

If you can learn to actively listen to what your customer tells you, you will have all the information you need to lead the conversation to a point where your customer will FEEL certain things that will result in the purchase decision.

Let's consider an example. Let's say John is a first-time homebuyer who has been looking at homes for a couple of months. You have helped him find one that both he and his wife like. He is approved for the loan but is concerned that the monthly payment will strain their household budget. John calls to tell you that he and his wife have decided to not buy the house.

SALESPERSON: I'm surprised to hear that, John. I remember when we first started working together that you said there were a number of goals you wanted to accomplish. Do you remember what those goals were?

JOHN: I know that in the long term, owning a house is better than renting. It's just that these interest rates put that payment a little higher than we're comfortable with right now. Maybe if we rented for another year, we could save more for the down payment.

Most sales training will tell you to focus on John's objections and attempt to overcome them. A couple of John's objections are:
- The payment is too high.
- The interest rate is too high.
- Their down payment is not big enough to reduce the monthly payment to where they would like it to be.
- In a year, (with presumably more money to put down) the payment will be lower.

Seasoned salespersons might see past these objections and wonder whether John and his wife really like the house. This can be inferred because the one thing John is not saying (maybe he doesn't even realize it himself) is the monthly cost to buy the house is higher than the perceived value of owning the house.

To counter John's objections, one option would be to share third-party information concerning forecasts for future interest rates and home values. If these third parties are trusted sources, John might conclude that it could cost more to buy the same house in a year.

Another option would be to throw a bunch of math at him. Projected rent minus projected house payment would represent the actual monthly savings if they continued to rent. Is that amount higher or lower than the projected equity gain if they owned the house for a year? (This analysis could also include the tax savings for mortgage interest and property tax deductions.)

The problem with sharing this kind of information is all of it is logical and we know that purchase decisions are made with the emotions. What we might try instead is to lead the conversation so John begins to talk about things that will make him feel a certain way.

SALESPERSON: John, I need to ask you. How much different do you think your life would be if you were able to accomplish those financial goals you had when we first started working together?

No matter what he says (even if he doesn't say anything at all) when the salesperson asks this question, John will now begin to feel what it would be like to accomplish his goals as opposed to what it would feel like to put them on hold.

No one wants to feel like they've failed at something. In fact, in a situation like this, the typical response is for John to minimize the importance of those original goals. From what he said earlier in the conversation, it sounds like he is already trying to justify not doing what it takes to achieve his goals.

If he can make those goals less important in his mind, it will be easier for him live with the decision to put his goals on hold. By asking him how it might FEEL to accomplish those goals, the salesperson is attempting to keep the goals in the forefront of John's mind. It's entirely up to John to decide how important those goals actually are.

Remember, the decision to spend money is always reserved for the customer. What we don't know is whether John's projected feeling of accomplishment will be strong enough to overcome his reluctance to pay the price to achieve his goals.

Also remember that when the perceived use-value is greater than the cost to buy, a sales transaction will take place every time. John will buy the house if his desire to feel that sense of accomplishment is worth more to him than the monthly payment.

6 - SECOND MOST VALUABLE ASSET

Once we learn how to communicate more effectively with customers, the next step is to find customers to communicate with. Even though there is a whole world full of strangers we could try to meet, why not start with people we already know?

Let's say you're thirty years old. You graduated high school, went to college, and have had three jobs since you were a teenager. Consider how many people you have met during the various stages of your educational/work journey. (This doesn't even include customers you may have interacted with if you worked in a restaurant or retail.) If you added them all up, the total would likely be in the thousands.

Let's say your number of previous friends and coworkers was only a couple of hundred. Let's also say you had a system in place to record and store full contact information for these people – name, address, email and phone number.

The term for this is your database, and you can store this information anywhere. Some of it is already right there on your phone. If you were to become purposeful about this though, that contact information could be consolidated and stored in one place. Ideally, you would also have the capacity to categorize and sort those contacts as well.

You can use something as simple as an Xcel spreadsheet, but I recommend you consider an online CRM (Customer Relationship Management) system. Most of them have free versions available and since you're only collecting and categorizing the information at this point, you likely won't need any of the advanced features in the paid plans.

You also might consider a CRM that offers sync capabilities. The way this works is once the sync relationship is established, all the information that is currently in your phone and/or email contacts would automatically be populated into your CRM system and updated (if there were any changes.)

No matter what system you decide to use to store and categorize the contacts, let's say you accept a position selling some kind of consumer product – electronics, computers, cars or even houses. How valuable do you think all that contact information would be then?

Do you remember our example about trust from chapter two? Megan had a pre-existing relationship with Susan and because they were friends, they had established a level of trust. Megan could leverage that trust to initiate a conversation and potentially make product or service recommendations.

Let's be realistic. You won't magically create a sale by simply having someone's contact information. As an example, let's say Franco sat across from you in Chemistry class in the 11th grade but you haven't talked to him since high school. If you call him up ten years later and start pitching the features and benefits of the product or service you're selling, you likely won't be any more trustworthy than the telemarketer who cold calls Franco.

Just because you once knew someone doesn't mean they

will trust you indefinitely, (or even remember you.) But if you had their contact information and developed a system to stay in touch (in a non-sales capacity) you would substantially increase the probability of converting that person to a customer at some point in the future.

In the digital world, we have things like smart phones and social media.

- What happens to the contacts in your phone when you upgrade to the latest model? They are automatically transferred to your new phone.
- What happens to your social media contacts if you change jobs and move to a new state? Absolutely nothing. You are still connected with all those people on the social media platform.

If you're beginning to understand the value of having a database and have begun the process of consolidating, categorizing, and sorting your contacts, the next question would be how can you stay in touch with them in a systematized way?

The easiest way to get started is birthdays and holidays. Facebook provides the option of publishing your birthday (with or without the year.) Not everyone shares that information but if you're friends with someone who does, Facebook will give you a popup notification on your friend's birthday. All you need to do is write a quick message, click the button and the message is posted on that person's timeline.

Since your friend's privacy settings make the birthday visible, you could add the information into your CRM (or sync it if the CRM provides that option.) You might also consider adding other important dates for the contact, such as children's birthdays, wedding anniversaries, or any other meaningful or significant date.

A holiday is much easier since it's the same day for

everyone. When sending holiday messages, try to avoid any unintended interpretations. I personally avoid sending "Merry Christmas" messages to those I know who are Jewish or Muslim. More secular messaging such as "Happy Holidays" tends to minimize the risk of offending anyone.

If you wanted to, you could find a holiday for every month of the year, but then you might wonder if sending a holiday greeting every month would be too much. If we look to successful sales organizations for guidance, we can find multiple examples that suggest there is no such thing as over-communicating with prospects or customers.

In the early days of Dell Computer, the company built its business with magazine advertisements, but those ads were only seen by the people who read the magazines. As the company grew, the marketing department began mailing out product brochures to businesses. If someone registered a new business, Dell got their address and mailed a brochure. Everyone from the sole proprietor selling products on eBay to the multi-national corporation opening a new sales office, got a Dell product brochure.

Very few companies have that kind of budget for postage, and I'm not suggesting you go into debt mailing holiday cards to people you may not even be selling to yet. What I am suggesting is you understand that if the goal is to stay top of mind, then you must BLAST your way inside the mind of your prospect or customer.

One way to do that is to implement a systematized and ECONOMICAL way of staying in touch with your database on a regular basis. Let's say you've consolidated those couple of hundred contacts into your CRM, and then you decide to implement a birthday/holiday strategy. It could be cost prohibitive to mail something every month, but what about a less expensive (or no cost) ways of communicating the same message?

You could send a text, email or Facebook message and it wouldn't cost you anything except the time required to send it. If all of them went out on the day of the holiday, it might take a while to send a couple hundred individual texts. If you were willing to invest a little bit of money, one solution would be an app that gave you the ability to send mass texts. The cost for something like this would be substantially less than the cost of the postage to mail the same number of cards.

Also remember that a phone call, (voice to voice communication,) is by far the most effective way to stay in touch with your contacts. This can be somewhat challenging if you have a large database and are not currently selling to these contacts. One solution would be to call a small number of your contacts every week and after you've worked through the database, (or a shorter list of VIP contacts,) you could start back at the top of the list again.

The only wrong way to communicate with your database is to not communicate at all. Consider the example of Franco earlier in this chapter. You may have talked to him every day during class in the 11th grade, but ten years later, he may not even remember who you are.

If the only thing you did was post a "Happy Birthday" message on Franco's Facebook timeline every year, he might still remember you ten years later. Imagine how much more likely it would be that he remembered you if you had sent some type of holiday greeting every month for ten years?

It bears repeating, if the goal is to stay top of mind, you must BLAST your way inside the mind of your prospect or customer.

Another thing to remember is your database is constantly growing and changing. If you took a sales position selling high-end items like Rolex watches or Mercedes Benz cars but your database was full of contacts who couldn't afford those products, you likely would prioritize meeting and adding new contacts who were more qualified. Does that mean you ignore the less qualified contacts who have been in your database for years?

That's totally up to you. If all you're doing is sending a couple of periodic text messages, it may not require a substantial amount of time or money to continue doing that. Remember this though. We often assume that whatever we're selling today is the same thing we will be selling in ten years. What happens if an opportunity presents itself where those unqualified contacts suddenly become more valuable?

- After several years selling Rolex watches, you decide to buy a pawn shop.
- You become one of the top salespeople at Mercedes Benz and are offered a management opportunity at a Ford dealership.

In both of these examples, the contacts who weren't qualified to buy the high-end items are now sales prospects in your new position. If you failed to keep in touch with them, you could find yourself needing to reestablish the connection. If it's been too long, you may not even have accurate contact information anymore.

This also highlights the importance of having the capacity to categorize and sort your contacts. If all you have are names and phone numbers in your phone and you decided to reach out to previous friends or coworkers who might want to buy a Rolex, you might be challenged figuring out where to start. If those same contacts were in a CRM system that offered tagging and categorizing options, it would be much easier to segment and subdivide your database to create meaningful subsets.

In summary, the purpose of this chapter is not to provide in-depth instructions on how to create, manage and market to a database. The sole purpose is to highlight the importance of creating a systematized approach to managing and marketing to your contacts.

Your database represents RELATIONSHIPS you have established with people who you've built a level of trust with. As you begin to understand how valuable this asset is, you should also begin to give it the attention it deserves.

Have you ever considered what assets are exchanged when a business is sold? Yes, the new owner will get the building, the inventory, the receivables and all the other assets, but the most valuable asset they get is the database.

You should begin to view yourself as a business that provides sales services – even if you're a W-2 employee. When you do this, you'll clearly understand the importance of your two most valuable assets.

- Your ability to communicate effectively with customers.
- The relationships you've established with people you've built a level of trust with. Another term for this is your database.

You'll take your ability to communicate with you no matter where you go, but what about your database? When you take ownership of it by managing and marketing to it, it becomes portable. In other words, you'll be able to take it with you if you change jobs or start a business.

7 - THE SALES PROCESS

We have now identified the two most valuable assets of any salesperson.
- The ability to effectively communicate.
- A database of contacts you've established some level of trust with, along with a systematized method of regularly communicating with that database.

These are the tools the salesperson will bring to the sales process. There are four stages to the sales process and the next four chapters will examine each one in depth. For review, the four steps of the sales process are:

1. Awareness of Need
2. Identify Options
3. Select Best Value
4. Finalize Purchase

After we analyze these individual steps, it will become easier to identify where customers might be in the sales process. Since customers will be looking for different things in each stage, our primary purpose is to understand two things.

- What are customers looking for in each stage?
- What should a salesperson focus on providing customers in each stage?

8 - AWARENESS OF NEED

Let's start by defining what a "need" is. Specifically, how a need is interconnected to a want. I think we can agree that there is a difference between wanting something and needing something, but it's also important to understand there are various degrees of want. In fact, it might be helpful to categorize wants into one of two categories.

- An underlying want is theoretical because it may not ever go any further than a thought.
- A motivating want compels someone to take action. In the sales process, this is when a customer wants a product or service so much that they buy it.

You may have heard Maslow's theory about the hierarchy of needs. (See the drawing on the next page.) Simply stated, there are levels of needs, and a person is not concerned with the higher-level needs until after the lower-level ones are satisfied. It's often diagramed as a pyramid and at the base are our basic needs, such as food, clothing, and shelter.

Once those basis needs are satisfied, the person moves to the next level, which is the need for safety. After that comes love and belonging needs, then esteem, and finally at the top of the pyramid, is transcendence or spirituality.

Maslow's theory makes sense and is applicable to the sales process. Consider the high-end luxury items we discussed in the chapter about your database. A qualified customer for a Rolex watch or Mercedes Benz car will already have satisfied lower-level needs such as the need for financial security. A customer who has not yet satisfied those lower-level needs may aspire to buy one of those luxury items but wouldn't be able to until after the lower-level needs were satisfied.

One thing Maslow's theory does not take into account is that a need doesn't exist unless there is an underlying want. Consider the basic need for food. Yes, we all need food in order to live, but what happens if someone doesn't WANT to live? This person is depressed, has lost hope, and sees no reason to go on. The underlying want is gone, so the need would no longer exist, (or at least the person's perception of the importance of that need wouldn't exist.)

It's debatable whether the need for food would truly disappear, but I'll leave that for the psychiatrists and psychologists to figure out. In our discussion we are focused exclusively on the sales process, and within the confines of sales, this model is 100% accurate.

As a salesperson, it is critical that you understand this.

Let's consider an example. Let's say someone wants a job. This is an underlying want which that person may or may not ever act on. If that underlying want evolved into an awareness of a need, it might progress something like this.

- The person wants a job.
- A thought comes to that person (heavily influenced by multiple marketing messages) that one way to satisfy that need would be to buy a car, since a car would enable that person to drive to the interview and back and forth to work after the job was secured.
- The underlying want evolved into an awareness of the need for a car.
- The person thus begins the sales process and might eventually buy a car.

Here's another example.

- Someone wants to lose some weight and adopt a healthier lifestyle.
- A thought comes to that person (after years of subliminal marketing messages from a variety of media sources) that a couple of ways to satisfy those wants are to

join a gym, change eating habits, or maybe hire a personal trainer.
- This underlying want evolved into an awareness of the need for a gym membership, organic food, and personal training services.
- The person begins the sales process and might eventually buy these things.

As you reflect on this, you'll see that this model applies to the sales process for every type of product or service. In fact, it is the foundation of the sales process.

If you want to be an effective salesperson, it is critical that you understand your customer's underlying wants. They are the primary motivation behind all the customer's actions (or inactions) during the sales process. Here are a couple of additional things to remember.

- The underlying want is not directly related to the product or service UNTIL that product or service is perceived as a way to satisfy the underlying want. In other words, the product or service is a solution to a problem – the customer has an unfulfilled want and begins to look for ways to satisfy it.
- The movement to the awareness of the need is a logical process, but the customer's ability to move through the remaining steps of the sales process will be determined by the amount of emotion attached to that underlying want. If the desire to satisfy the underlying want begins to fade, the customer could lose interest in continuing the sales process and might never purchase the product or service.
- The underlying want could remain unsatisfied for a long time. The customer may never act on it, or as we mentioned earlier, lose interest and either pause or stop the sales process.
- If a customer does pause or stop the sales process, that person could revisit, resume, or restart it at any time –

BUT ONLY AFTER the emotions attached to the underlying want were amplified.

The awareness of need must happen before the sales process can begin, and since it is only the first step of the sales process, the salesperson should only be focused on two things.

- Amplifying the emotions which are attached to the customer's underlying want.
- Moving the customer to the next step of the sales process by positioning the product or service as the perfect way to satisfy the underlying want.

Once the salesperson begins educating the customer about the features and benefits of the product or service, the customer has moved to the second step of the sales process, which is Identify Options.

9 - IDENTIFY OPTIONS

This is the stage of the sales process where salespeople first meet prospective customers. There are some exceptions, particularly if the salesperson is engaged in prospecting or lead generation, but when customers begin to identify and compare options, they have entered the stage where they need something (brochure or website) or someone (salesperson) to educate them on the features and benefits of the product or service.

Everything we previously discussed about establishing trust becomes critical in this stage. You might be the most knowledgeable salesperson in the entire company. You might know many details about your product. You might also know details about the competitor's product and can provide graphs, charts and supporting materials which compare the features and benefits.

All of this is important, but if customers don't trust you, they'll never believe you, which means they'll probably never buy from you – UNLESS you can overcome this. If you haven't yet earned the customer's trust, one way you can still persuade is to quote the opinions of respected authorities.

If this is done effectively, it separates you from the information. You become the messenger who is delivering someone else's message. That message can be very persuasive if your customer recognizes the information source as a trusted authority. To do this, you'll preface your statements like this:

- "According to (the respected authority,) ..."
- "(The respected authority) recently did a product comparison and their research showed ..."
- "I used to think that too, but then I read an article by (the respected authority) which said ..."

The internet is full of information sources you can draw from but be aware that some are more respected than others, which will make them more credible – and thus more persuasive. If you were selling cars, your personal opinion would be the least credible. Information provided by the manufacturer would be slightly better, but a review from a third-party news outlet, like *Car & Driver Magazine*, would be the best.

A third party has no vested interest in whether or not their information helps to sell the product or service. At least that should be the customer's perception. Also, if one third party opinion is good then several are better, especially if they all reach the same conclusion.

If you are going to use third party opinions, it's important to be able to quote not only what was said, but who said it and when they said it. If you quote the opinion of a third party which was published ten years ago, it wouldn't be nearly as effective as something that was published last month.

The final thing to consider when using third party opinions is your customer's personality type will determine what kind of information will be the most persuasive. To better understand how this works, let's briefly discuss the

DISC personality model.

The DISC test (also known as a DISC assessment) is based on the DISC model and personality theory of psychologist Dr. William Moulton Marston. It has been adapted over time and today, you can find numerous websites which offer free assessments. You might consider taking one of these assessments to gain a better understanding of your own personality type.

The DISC model identifies four personality types. Although a formal assessment will provide more detail and a better understanding, this DISC model is not overly complicated. In fact, most people will be able to sense their own personality type and begin to identify the personality types of others after reading the following descriptions.

Dominant: This personality type relates to power, control, and assertiveness. Some adjectives used to describe a Dominant include direct, decisive, risk-taker, problem solver, and argumentative.

Influencer: This personality type relates to communication and social situations. Some adjectives used to describe an Influencer include outgoing, enthusiastic, optimistic, persuasive, impulsive, and emotional.

Steady: This personality type relates to patience, thoughtfulness, and stability. Some adjectives used to describe a Steady personality include good listener, predictable, understanding, supportive, friendly, and generous.

Compliant: This personality type relates to structure and organization. Some adjectives used to describe a Compliant personality include accurate, precise, careful, correct, systematic, analytical, and high standards.

An understanding of personality types will provide several tools which can enable salespeople to become more persuasive. Instead of relying exclusively on their own natural personality characteristics, salespeople can adapt to the customer's personality type and modify how information is presented. This gives salespeople choices in how they interact with customers.

The first thing to recognize is that very few people exhibit the characteristics of only one personality type. In fact, most of us have characteristics from each of them. All of us though, will have one that is the most prominent with a second that is complimentary.

Two of the most common combinations are the Dominant-Influencer and the Compliant-Steady. A true Dominant is a borderline sociopath. Someone with this personality type is highly intelligent and trusts his/her instincts. Dominants are natural leaders and won't hesitate to confront anyone who challenges them.

The Dominant-Influencer combination pairs assertiveness and control with communication and social skills. People with this combination of personality traits tend to succeed in most things they undertake. These are the CEO's and the entrepreneurs. This personality type also tends to do very well in sales.

On the other end of the spectrum is the Compliant-Steady, which pairs structure and organization with patience and stability. These are the engineers and technicians who work out the details of the Dominant-Influencer's grand plan. While Dominant-Influencers make decisions quickly, take action and prefer to work out the details later, Compliant-Steadies want to gather all the data, analyze it and will avoid taking action until they're convinced the plan will work.

Another thing to be aware of is certain personality types tend to clash with others. As discussed earlier, a Dominant-Influencer makes decisions quickly and is willing to take risks, while a Compliant-Steady is risk averse and "doesn't want to rock the boat."

If you were a salesperson with a Dominant-Influencer personality, a customer with a Compliant-Steady personality might perceive you as wanting to move too fast. If that customer felt rushed to make a decision, they would feel like you're using "high pressure" sales techniques, shut down and not buy from you.

A Compliant-Steady personality is thoughtful, patient and fears making a mistake. This type of person would rather delay making a decision than make the wrong one. If the salesperson was able to recognize the customer's Compliant-Steady personality, it would be possible to adapt the sales message to match the customer's personality type.

If you knew your customer preferred to move slowly and would become afraid if they felt pressured, wouldn't it make sense to slow down and try to make the customer feel more comfortable and secure? If you knew your customer was risk averse, wouldn't it make sense to position your product or service as a low-risk alternative that countless other people have chosen over the competitor's offerings?

Now that we have a basic understanding of personality types, let's combine it with some of the things we discussed earlier about third-party opinions. If we recognize that our customer is a Compliant-Steady, we know that person needs data to justify any purchase decision. Unless you are perceived as a subject matter expert, avoid telling this type of customer what you think. Instead, give that customer reams of data, spreadsheets, and the opinions of experts.

Compliant-Steadies are not going to make a quick decision, so incentives and objection handlers won't be effective. What can be effective though, is to meet them on their level and progress at their pace.

They seek structure and stability, so they will be loyal to you, but only if you play by their rules. If you slow down and give them all the data they ask for, you will establish a connection with them, which creates a sense of structure. Don't pressure them to make a decision but invite them to contact you if they require any additional information. Rarely, will they spend a lot of time gathering information with one salesperson and then go somewhere else after they've made the purchase decision.

Dominant-Influencers are just the opposite. They'll make a quick decision and won't be intimated if you apply a little pressure. You can ask them, "What would need to happen for you to make the decision to buy right now?"

They still might not buy from you, but customers with this personality type aren't afraid of confrontation. In fact, they might perceive you as weak if you don't try to close them. They also will feel the least loyalty to a specific salesperson or a brand. They'll make excessive demands on your time, furiously negotiate terms, promise to come see you once they've made a decision, and then go buy from someone else five minutes after leaving your office.

Third party opinions are not effective with Dominant-Influencers. Customers with this personality type trust their own instincts and don't need someone else to assure them they're making the right decision. The one exception is celebrity endorsements, particularly if that celebrity is successful in business. That Dominant-Influencer might not care what Lebron James says about your product or service, but an endorsement from someone like Elon Musk could have an impact.

One personality type we haven't discussed yet is the Influencer. You might see combinations such as Influencer-Dominant or Influencer-Compliant, but the most common is the Influencer-Steady.

These are the social butterflies. They crave interaction with others and because of their Compliant characteristics, they don't like to offend anyone. In other words, they want to be friends with everybody, and will become very uncomfortable if anyone disagrees with them. They avoid confrontation at all costs and want everyone in their social circle to get along.

The online review system was created for this personality type. They have active accounts on all the review sites and when they're in the market to buy something, they'll read everybody else's opinion about the product or service they're interested in. While data and expert opinions will be effective for Compliant-Steadies, Influencer-Steadies want to know what other customers think about your product or service.

With an understanding of personality types and third-party opinions, we can now define what the salesperson's strategy should be during the Identify Options stage of the sales process. Customers will tell you (and might actually believe) that all they want is information. They know they have a need for a specific type of product or service and will tell you they are "doing their research" to see what is available.

You, as the salesperson, must realize that this is not true. What customers really want in this stage is a reason to buy. They've already acknowledged they have a need a product or service like yours and could probably get all the information required to make a purchase decision online. In fact, in today's digital world there is a way to buy virtually any product or service without any human interaction.

But instead of doing that, they're coming to you. They need you for something and you must understand what they really want from you. They want you to convince them that your product or service is the best solution to solve their problem. Everything you do or say should be focused on helping them answer these three questions.

- Does your product or service solve their problem?

- Is it the best solution to solve that problem?
- Is solving that problem more valuable than the cost to buy your product or service?

In other words, Identify Options and Select Best Value are two separate stages of the sales process, but they do not exist independently. A customer wants to think they do, but the salesperson must combine them. Everything about your sales presentation should do two things simultaneously.

- Provide information about your product or service in the most persuasive way based on the customer's personality type.
- Position your product or service as the best value so it's easy for the customer to choose to buy it.

10 - SELECT BEST VALUE

Since your objective as a salesperson is to combine the Identify Options and Select Best Value stages of the sales process, any time you're interacting with a customer your focus should be to uncover the true answer to this question.

What are the reasons this customer has not yet decided to buy my product or service?

Let's first examine what a "true" answer is. If you have established a level of trust with your customer and have some rapport, you could ask a direct question like, "Why haven't you bought yet?"

The problem with asking a question like this is the customer will never give you the real reason. Most times, that customer doesn't even know the answer. What the customer will do is rattle off a number of meaningless responses designed to shield and protect them from "being sold." In other words, buying something the customer doesn't want or making a bad decision. These responses usually go something like this.

- "I'm not buying today."
- "I'm just looking."

- "I've got plenty of time to make a decision."

As discussed in the previous chapter, you as the salesperson must recognize that the customer would not be talking to you unless they wanted to buy. Of course, there will be times when a customer might have the desire to buy but isn't qualified to buy, so you should have some type of process to uncover this early. You certainly don't want to spend an excessive amount of time with someone who doesn't have the ability to buy your product or service.

Let's say you've qualified your customer and are now attempting to uncover the reasons why they haven't bought yet. Since that customer will never tell you the true reason (they probably don't even know), you need to act like a detective and search for clues. Your ability to read the signs the customer is giving you will determine what aspects of the features and benefits you'll need to highlight.

Most times, the reasons the customer hasn't bought yet is because they don't know something about one of these things.

- How will your product or service benefit the customer (solve a problem.)
- How do the features and benefits of your product or service compare with the competitor's offerings.
- How is the use-value of your product or service more valuable than the cost to buy it.
- How is the use-value of your product or service more valuable than the use-value of the competitor's product or service. (Even if your price is higher, how is your product or service a better value.)

Remember this. Customers don't change their minds. They make new decisions based on new information. Your goal should be to provide the RIGHT new information, so the customer makes the decision to buy your product or service.

As discussed in previous chapters, your effectiveness as a salesperson will be determined by the quality of the questions you ask and your ability to shut up and listen to what the customer tells you. In other words, you need to ask questions to find out what information the customer wants from you, but how you ask those questions will determine how much the customer will reveal to you.

Consider what it would be like to be a suspect in a television police drama like *Law & Order*. You're locked in a room and the detectives start firing off questions at you. They are trying to get you to either admit that you did it or find holes in your story. Very quickly, you would feel like you're being attacked and become defensive.

You certainly don't want your customers to feel like this when you ask them questions. You're not interrogating them. You're trying to have a conversation with them. Here are two important things you should learn to do when structuring the questions to ask your customers.

- Ask open ended questions.
- Preface your questions.

Any question that can be answered yes/no is closed ended. Since your goal is to get your customer to open up and give you information which you can use to position your product or service, you'll want to ask questions that encourage your customer to talk. Here are a couple of examples.

- Closed ended: "Have you looked at any of the competitor's products yet?"
- Open ended: "What other products are you considering?"

- Closed ended: "Do you know when you will be making a decision?
- Open ended: "What are some things that might

impact your purchase timeline?

- Closed ended: "Are you ready to buy today?"
- Open ended: "If we found a product that met all your needs and the price was agreeable to you, what are some of the other things we'll need to address before we can complete the sale?

Prefacing means that you tell the customer why you're asking the question and then ask the question. This technique will minimize the risk of customers feeling like you're interrogating them. Here are a couple of examples.

- "So that I can better understand your needs and make more meaningful suggestions, I was curious what type of research have you done already about our products or services?"
- "In order for me to more effectively help you and to save you time, can you help me understand what you're trying to accomplish today?"
- "My goal is to help you make the best decision, so I want to make sure you have all the information you need to accomplish that. Based on what you know about our products already, what types of questions or concerns do you have about whether our products are the best solution for you?"

As you learn to ask more effective questions, you must also train yourself to become a better listener. This means you need to stop thinking about how you're going to respond and actively listen to what your customer tells you. Don't assume you know what your customer means because you can't see things from their perspective.

One effective way to ensure you're understanding your customer is to repeat back what you've heard. When you learn to do this, it will also reassure your customer that they are being heard. Have you ever been in a conversation where it felt like the other person wasn't hearing what you were trying to say? Well, you never want your customer to feel like that.

When your customer tells you something or answers one of your questions, listen and then respond like this.

- "If I'm hearing your correctly, (whatever the customer just said.)"
- "So, what you're saying is (whatever the customer just said.)"
- "If I understand what you're saying, (whatever the customer just said.)"

Once you've clarified and confirmed what the customer is telling you, the final step is to use that information to position your product or service. If the customer is concerned about the price, you need to demonstrate how the use-value of your product or service is more valuable than the cost. If the customer says the competitor's product is a better value, you need to provide evidence which challenges that (review the section on third-party opinions and personality types so your response is persuasive.)

The information you provide will be based on what you know about the features and benefits of your product or service. The structure of how you present that information should be guided by these two rules.

- Always agree with your customer.
- Eliminate the word "but" from your vocabulary.

A debate is often confrontational. The interchange usually goes something like this. The first person states an opinion and then the second person says something to the effect of, "Your opinion is not correct. Let me tell you why you're wrong and I'm right."

If you debate with your customers, you'll never win the argument. You might have better supporting data and you may very well be right, but if you tell customers they're wrong, they'll put up defenses and won't listen to you. They'll cling to their opinion and protect it like a medieval army protects a castle. This is not how you persuade someone.

What you want to do instead is agree with them. First of all, they're not expecting it. Most people already have their defenses up when they talk to salespeople because they don't want to be "sold." When you agree with your customers, they'll let down their guard just a little bit.

Secondly, something happens psychology when someone agrees with us. A connection is established, and we have positive feelings towards that person. These are the exact types of feelings you want your customers to feel towards you. When your customer feels like that, you become more likeable and more worthy of that customer's trust.

No matter what your customer says, (even if you think the customer's statement is not correct,) learn to immediately respond like this.

- "You're right."
- "I can agree with that."
- "That is true."

The next word you say is more important than anything else. You have the entire English language to choose from and there is only one word you should never use. Never, under any circumstances, agree with your customer and then say "but."

If you say "but," you completely negate everything that came before it. Which also means you negate all those positive feelings your customer just felt towards you. Think about how you feel when someone uses a "but" statement on you.

- You've been dating someone and you're having a romantic dinner together. Your love interest looks into your eyes and says, "I really like you and I've had so much fun

spending time with you, BUT ..."
- You interview for a job and the hiring manager says, "I like everything I see on this resume, and you seem like a person who would do well here, BUT ..."
- You've spent the last two weeks following up with a customer and providing every last shred of data and supporting documentation that's been requested. The customer calls you and says, "I really like your product and I appreciate all the time you've invested in helping me understand the features and benefits, BUT ..."

That "but" means bad news is coming. Anybody on the receiving end of a "but" statement will instantly prepare to be let down. That person anticipates whatever comes next will be some kind of objection, criticism, or other disappointing news. That person knows the conversation has just taken a turn and the one receiving the "but" is not going to be happy with how it all ends.

You do not want your customer to feel like this, so don't use the word "but." Here are a couple of alternatives.
- "I completely agree with you. I've read that same analysis and that respected authority brings up a number of good points. I don't know if you've seen this other article by another respected authority where many of the theories in that first article were shown to be untrue."
- "It is true that the competitor makes a very good product. That's one of the reasons they sell so many of them. One thing they probably won't tell you though is that two of their biggest customer complaints are ..."
- "I can agree with that. It sounds like you've done a lot of research on this. I would assume that someone like yourself would want to make sure they have all the information before making a decision. Let me show you something that you'll probably find very interesting."

The final thing we need to discuss for this stage of the

sales process is overcoming objections. There are a lot of inexperienced salespeople out there, (and a lot of sales trainers,) who will have you believe that overcoming objections is about learning clever phrases that can somehow trick customers into changing their minds.

These objection handlers can be entertaining and might work one time out of a thousand tries, but most times a customer will see right through them. They may have worked back in the days of the snake oil salesmen, but today's customers are much more sophisticated. Many times, your customers are going to be smarter than you are and might even know more about your products and services than you do. If you think you're going to trick them with some kind of verbal gymnastics, you're going to be disappointed with your results.

What overcoming objections is really about is finding the answers to the question we asked at the beginning of this chapter.

What are the reasons this customer has not yet decided to buy my product or service?

Remember, you should be looking for the "true" reasons. That customer might tell you, "I need to think about it," or "I need to talk to my wife," or "I'm not sure if this is the right time," but it's highly unlikely that any of those are the true reasons. You must use all the tools we've discussed in this chapter to get your customer to open up and reveal what those true reasons are.

That customer may not tell you directly, but if you listen and look for the clues, you can uncover them. In fact, you might discover the true reasons before your customer realizes what they are.

Overcoming objections is like helping your customer solve a problem. Here are a couple of examples.

- If the price is too high, how can we find financing

alternatives which will make the purchase more affordable?

- If the customer wants to wait, how can we quantify the hidden costs associated with delaying the purchase for six months or a year?
- If the customer prefers the competitor's product or service, how can we reexamine the features and benefits of your product or service so the customer can revalue it? (Hopefully, higher than before.)

Ultimately, the customer is going to make a decision, and no matter what that decision is, the sales process will then move to the fourth and final stage, Finalize Purchase.

11 - FINALIZE PURCHASE

Let's review some of the things we've discussed so far. After a customer becomes aware of the need for specific type of product or service, they will begin to explore and identify options. This is usually when that customer first meets the salesperson. The customer might think this is a time for gathering information and "doing research," but the salesperson knows that at this point, the customer is actually searching for reasons to buy the product or service.

The salesperson will educate the customer on the features and benefits of the product or service and position it as both the best solution and the best value when compared to the offerings of the competitors. Of all the products and services available (or at least the ones the customer is aware of), that customer will eventually choose the one they think is the best value.

The salesperson will use a number of tools to persuade the customer and influence that final decision, including the use of third-party opinions, providing the most persuasive information based on the customer's personality type and structuring questions and responses in ways designed to make the customers feel more favorable emotions towards both the salesperson and the products and services being offered.

After all of this, the salesperson will ask the customer to make a decision. The salesperson will invite the customer to do business together. When the salesperson asks, "Do you want to buy my product or service?" the customer will respond with one of three answers.

- "Yes." The customer purchases the product or service.
- "No." The customer purchases the competitor's product or service.
- "Maybe later." The customer decides not to make any purchase at this time.

If the customer chooses to buy your product or service, all you need to do is finalize the transaction and thank the customer for their business. Once the sale is complete, you also need to realize your relationship with that customer is not over. In fact, it has just begun. That customer can become a source for future repeat and referral business, but only if you have some type of follow-up system in place.

This could be as simple as a periodic check-in to see if the customer is still enjoying the product or service and whether any questions or concerns may have come up. (You might want to review the chapter on managing and marketing to a database for ideas on how you might integrate these sold customers into your campaigns.)

Remember, your database represents relationships, and an ongoing relationship with a previous customer can be one of your most valuable relationships because it can lead to many additional sales. For one thing, it is much easier to sell to someone who has already bought from you than it is to sell to a stranger you just met.

If your customer bought an expensive item like a house

or a car, they may not be in the market again for several years. A customer who bought a vacation package or accounting services though, could come back to you and buy again more frequently. No matter what the sales cycle might be for your product or service, every one of your previous customers has family, friends and co-workers who may have a need for your product or service at some point in the future.

If you remember everything we've talked about concerning the importance of trust, consider the power of a personal recommendation. If your previous customer recommends you to a friend, family member or co-worker, that person will trust you before they even meet you. It will be almost as easy to sell to that person as it would to sell to the previous customer you have the existing relationship with.

When you treat your previous customers as lead sources, it should become clear that the initial sale could very well be just the beginning of a number of sales over the next several months or years. Those sales could be yours, if you periodically follow-up with your previous customers and ask them, "Do you know anyone who might have a need for my products or services?"

But what if the customer chooses not to buy your product or service, and buys from your competitor instead? Does that mean you should ignore that customer? As your database grows, you will begin to make choices about which category of contacts are your highest priority. You might decide that someone who didn't buy from you is a lower priority contact, but that doesn't mean the person can't be added to some type of automated follow-up, such as an email newsletter or a holiday text campaign.

This type of strategy would be most effective (and compliant with anti-SPAM laws) if you initiated it soon after your initial interaction with the customer. If you retained the customer's contact information in your database and suddenly start sending email newsletters five years after your sales presentation, that person might perceive your emails as SPAM. This means it would be highly recommended that you gain an understanding of federal, state, and local restrictions on unsolicited marketing emails and texts before launching any campaigns.

The final possible result you might experience after taking a customer through the sales process, is the customer decides not to buy anything. For follow up purposes, this type of customer will probably be a higher priority contact than the one who bought from the competitor, but part of that will depend on the reason the customer chose not to buy.

There are legitimate objections to making a purchase. An example would be that the customer was laid off from work and lost their primary source of income. That customer won't be in the market for your product or service until the employment status improves. There is nothing the salesperson can do to change the customer's situation, so the salesperson would need to be patient, follow up occasionally, and wait until the customer became ready to revisit the possibility of buying your product or service.

Most times though, the objection to buying will be because the customer's perceived needs have changed. (You might revisit the chapter which discussed the inter-relationship between the customer's underlying want and the need for your product or service.)

More than likely, the customer chooses not to buy because the emotions attached to the underlying want have begun to fade. The salesperson could attempt to amplify the emotions attached to the underlying want, but sometimes customers figure out that they just don't feel as strongly about that underlying want as they did when they first started shopping. If that's the case, there's little the salesperson can do to change things.

The type and frequency of follow up for this type of unsold customer will depend on the priority the salesperson assigns to them. There are some who advocate the strategy of following up with every single customer "until they buy or die," but that may not be the most efficient use of a salesperson's time.

The Pareto principle tells us that roughly 80% of your sales results will come from 20% of the actions you take. On one hand, you never know how a customer's situation might change over time. If you follow up with everyone regardless of whether or not you think they're ever going to buy, you will substantially increase the likelihood of finding sales in those unsold leads.

On the other hand, what if the salesperson has better results talking with new customers who have just begun the sales process? Would it make much sense to spend a lot of time trying to find customers who might have changed their mind when there are fresh customers wanting information about your product or service?

I'll attempt to answer these questions and conclude our discussion of the sales process with the following thoughts. You have the exact same amount of time available in each day as every other person on this planet. How you choose to use that time will determine the results you will see at the end of the day.

Your work ethic will determine how much of that available time you're willing spend on work-related tasks. When you first start in a new sales position, you might find yourself spending a larger portion of your day on work-related tasks, as you learn about the products and services and the company's internal systems and processes. With time and experience, you will discover which types of work-related tasks enable you to produce the best results.

If you focus on working hard, you will find more difficult things to do – and they will keep you busy. If you focus on efficiency and results, you will find more efficient ways to produce results. You might even discover that you're able to produce the same results in less time than the "hard worker." Does that mean you need to readjust how you do things?

That might make sense if you were paid by the hour. That type of compensation plan does not incentivize efficiency. If the "hard worker" took eight hours to complete a task and you could do it in two, you would either be paid less (for only the two hours), or your supervisor would find additional tasks for you to complete.

In the world of sales, it's the complete opposite because efficiency is rewarded. Let's say that instead of being paid hourly, you are paid a flat commission on each sale. It takes you two hours to close a sale, but the "hard worker" needs eight hours. You both would earn the same amount of money for each sale, but you would have spent substantially less time to get the same result.

If you could maintain that same efficiency for an entire eight-hour workday, you would have four sales at the end of the day, while the "hard worker" would only have one. Since you are paid per sale, you would be rewarded in proportion to the results you produced. In this example, you would earn four times more income than the "hard worker."

"I choose a lazy person to do a hard job. Because a lazy person will find an easy way to do it."
- Bill Gates

12 - BEYOND POSITIVE THINKING

Many of the tasks associated with sales success involve doing repetitive, mundane, and sometimes even boring things. One example would be cold calling for new leads. It's repetitive – you will probably say the same thing on every call, and there is a lot of rejection – substantially more people will tell you "no" before you find one who will say "yes."

You might think it takes a special type of person to be able to persevere despite all this repetition and rejection. You will constantly encounter angry people who are mad just because you called, and they certainly don't want to talk to you. They might curse at you and hang up before you even get the chance to say why you're calling. Yet, the salesperson smiles and dials the next number with the same level of enthusiasm they had on the first call of the day.

The ability to do this on a regular basis, several hours a day, every day of the week, doesn't necessarily require a special type of person or any special talent. What it does require though, is a special type of mindset. It might take some focus and effort to learn how to adopt this mindset, but anyone can learn to do it.

A positive mental attitude is a concept first introduced by Napoleon Hill in the book, *Think and Grow Rich*. (If you haven't read this book already, it is highly advised that you do.) The term "positive thinking" is never actually used in the book, but the book does discuss how positive thinking is one the most important contributing factors to success.

The book was originally published in 1937 and since then, there have been numerous books written and published which also stress the importance of a positive mental attitude. Some equate positive thinking with optimism or focusing on the good in every situation, but it encompasses much more than that.

One of the key components is that if someone has a positive mental attitude, that person can accept both the good and the bad in life but has an expectation that things will go well. In fact, they are going to go exactly as the person wants them to.

"I can and I will get what I want," is an affirmation which embodies this.

If the salesperson from earlier in this chapter adopted a mental attitude like this, it would become easier to push through the repetition and rejection associated with cold calling, but would it be enough?

If the salesperson expects things to go well, that person could envision finding a new lead on every call. The salesperson might practice affirmations like, "they are waiting for me to call," or "this call will produce a new lead," but no matter how powerful the affirmation or how positive the salesperson's mental attitude, a lead from every call is not going to happen.

No matter what type of product or service is being sold, the type of call list being used, or the experience of the salesperson making the calls, there is a percentage which represents the ratio between the number of calls that must be made to produce a new lead. For our example, let's say it's ten percent. On average, for every ten calls the salesperson makes, they'll find one new lead. This means that nine out of every ten calls will say "no." Additionally, since this is an average, it might be possible to make twenty calls in a row and get a "no" every time, but then get two leads back-to-back on the next two calls.

But before making each call, the salesperson affirms, "this call will produce a new lead." Even though the salesperson envisions success and has positive expectations for success, the results the salesperson experiences don't match the affirmation. In fact, the growing body of evidence will suggest the affirmation is not true at all. This is reaffirmed call after call after call.

This is why it's so easy to become discouraged when doing repetitive sales tasks. That positive thinking might enable the salesperson to get started making the calls, but it won't be enough to sustain and motivate that person when everything screams that it's not working.

Part of the solution to this is to learn how to think bigger than the repetitive tasks in front of us. Consider this analogy. We are shipbuilders in the 1800's. Wood is only thing we have to work with, but with our tools and woodworking skills, we plan to build a ship that will take us around the world.

Building a ship is hard work and we must be exact in all our measurements. We would cut the wood with handsaws (no electric tools in the 1800's), we would hoist those massive blocks of wood with ropes and pulleys, and then piece everything together hoping it will all be sea-worthy when we're done. It will probably take over a year to complete the ship, so there will be many days when we might question whether we'll ever finish or whether all this work is going to be worth it.

The challenge we would face on a daily basis is to stay motivated. We could try to find motivation in the tasks we do each day. There is a certain sense of pride when a craftsman completes a task or figures out a solution. Maybe this could motivate us. We could focus on making every cut precise and hammer every nail perfectly.

This might work, but an alternative would be to visualize all the places this ship is going to take us when we're done. When we finish the ship and set sail, we could go to Egypt and see the Great Pyramids, or Africa and see all those exotic animals we've heard about. Or what about Greece, Italy or even China? This ship will enable us to explore the world and live a life of adventure.

Wouldn't you agree that focusing on what happens after the project is complete is much more emotionally charged? Wouldn't it be easier to get through the day-to-day challenges and disappointments when you knew they were nothing more than steps towards experiencing all those new places? Would it be possible to try something similar to this for our repetitive sales tasks?

Here's an example of how you might do that. Start with your income goal. It doesn't matter if you want to make a hundred thousand dollars, two hundred thousand dollars, or five hundred thousand dollars. Imagine what it will be like to achieve that goal. Are there specific things you want to buy? A house, car, or vacation? Don't visualize "a new car," but visualize a specific make and model, trim level, options, and color. Visualize that car parked in your driveway. Visualize driving it.

If you want that car, you'll need to hit your income goal, so you'll need to know how many sales it will take to get you there. Once you figure out how many sales you'll need, it should be easy to figure out how many new leads it would take to achieve that number of sales. After that, all you need to know is how many cold calls do you have to make to find that many new leads?

The example ratio we used for the number of calls required to produce one lead was ten-to-one. This means that nine out of every ten calls will result in a "no," but after that, we'll find the "yes." Now that you're visualizing the specific car you're going to buy when you hit your income goal, those "no's" become a necessary part of the process. In fact, the quicker you can get through those "no's," the quicker you'll find the lead, which means you'll be closer to the sale which is going to produce the income that's going to enable you to buy the car.

So, when you're making those calls and encountering all that rejection, your affirmation could be, "I want that car. I need those the "no's" to get it."

13 - TENACITY

Tenacity is defined as the quality displayed by someone who just won't quit, who keeps trying until they reach their goal. Most of us like to think we have tenacity, but if that were the case, everybody would enjoy massive success. The way it normally works is everyone starts with high expectations and great enthusiasm, but as obstacles present themselves and uncertainty creeps in, most people reach a point where THEY DECIDE it's not going to work, and they VOLUNTARILY stop pursuing their goal.

They'll blame other things for their failure to achieve the goal. They didn't have enough talent, education, or money. The market was down, or the timing was wrong. Maybe they were in the wrong city. If they changed locations, everything would be different. The problem with this kind of logic is that no matter what they might point to as the reason for their failure, there are examples of someone else achieving the same goal without having that very thing.

You can have excuses or you can have results, but you can't have both. If you haven't yet achieved your goal, there is nothing or no one you should blame except yourself. What are you not doing that you should be doing? What are you doing that should stop doing? What do you not know? What don't you know that you don't know?

Nothing in life is certain, but this is guaranteed – if you keep trying you will be ten thousand times more likely to achieve your goal than if you give up. Have the courage to set a goal so high that it scares you. Then reach down inside yourself and find the tenacity to do whatever it takes to achieve it.

A person with tenacity is dangerous because they're not swayed by all the shiny objects out there promising the quick fix or the easy way. Someone with tenacity knows what they want and stays focused on doing what it takes to get it. The entire world gets out of their way and falls in line.

Someone with tenacity knows that it's not the final blow that breaks the rock, but the thousand strikes that came before.

If someone truly had tenacity, that person would be extremely cautious when deciding what goal to pursue, because once the commitment was made, there would be no turning back.

I once heard a story about what Julius Caesar did when he led his troops across the English Channel to invade England. I have since learned that it may not have actually happened, but it's still a good story.

The Romans required ships to get across the English Channel, which is an arm of the Atlantic Ocean separating northern France from southern England. When Caesar's entire army had arrived on the English beach, he marched them up the first hill and ordered them to stop and turn around. As those soldiers looked out over the harbor, they saw that every single one of their ships was on fire.

Those soldiers had not been home in years. They had

followed Caesar across Europe, defeating everyone they encountered and expanding the Roman Empire. In those days, they had no contact with their loved ones back home when they were on a campaign. Children were born, children grew up and older relatives passed away. They missed all those life events because they had been fighting with Caesar for the glory of Rome.

Now, he wants to invade England. How long is that going to take? It could be another several years before they returned to Rome. As those ships burned in the harbor though, those soldiers instantly realized that their ONLY way home was forward. At its narrowest point, the English Channel is twenty-one miles across, so they won't be able to swim back. No. The only way back to Rome is to conquer England and take the English ships.

Caesar gave those soldiers the gift of tenacity because he took away every option except accomplishing the goal. There was no escape clause, contingency plan, or plan B. They were either going to conquer England and return home as heroes, or they would die there.

What normally happens when an individual or a group makes that level of commitment to accomplishing a goal? Without exception, they achieve it. Consider major accomplishments from history like the transcontinental railroad, or the creation of the atomic bomb, or even recently with the discovery of the COVID vaccine less than a year after the first case was reported. A group of people committed to doing something that had never been done before and they found a way to do it.

If you set a goal for yourself that you've never accomplished before, wouldn't you need the same level of commitment these people from history demonstrate? What are some ways you can ensure your commitment to your goals will keep you focused and motivated long enough to experience the joy of accomplishment?

One thing to be aware of is that sometimes it's possible to become committed to a method of accomplishing a goal and not recognize that you've lost sight of the actual goal. Does it really matter how you achieve a goal? Certainly, laws and morality will restrict some methods, but assuming it's legal and moral, which of the following has the highest chance of success?

- Doing it the way you think will work.
- Doing it the way the experts say will work.
- Constantly measuring, adapting, and adjusting until you find the way that works.

Here's another story for you. A bird saw a beautiful garden with an abundance of sun, food, and water. The problem was the bird was separated from that garden by a huge sheet of glass. Every day, the bird would fly towards the garden, slam into the glass and knock itself unconscious. The bird tried approaching it from different angles, different speeds, and different times of the day, but every attempt was the same result. The bird slammed into the glass and knocked itself unconscious.

One day, as the bird was waking up from its latest self-induced unconscious state, it stumbled about ten feet from where it had made its last attempt to fly into the garden. The bird couldn't believe what it saw. Right there in front of it was something that had been there the entire time. The bird shook its head in disbelief, but at the same time was so happy. Right there in front of it was an open door. The view of the garden was the same, whether through the door or through the glass, but once the bird found the door, all it had to do was walk right into the garden.

If you don't have tenacity, you need to get some.

14 - SPENDING THE MONEY

We previously discussed some of the differences between getting paid for your time versus paid for results. If someone is paid by the hour, there is no incentive to be efficient. In fact, the longer it takes to complete a task, the more money that person will make. If the job takes longer than planned and the person is asked to work extra hours, they'll expect even more money, in the form of overtime pay.

This method of compensation is used in a wide range of industries and does offer some advantages. First, the employee assumes no risk with respect to the effectiveness of the tasks they are paid to do. Let's say the employee spends several weeks working on a marketing campaign designed to attract new customers. The campaign is launched, and it results in zero new leads. That employee would still expect to be paid for their time.

Another advantage is that it's very easy for an employee to plan and forecast personal finances. Paydays are scheduled on the calendar and the employee will expect to receive a certain amount of money on each of those days.

There might be some fluctuations in the amount, depending on overtime and bonuses, but for the most part, the employee will know how much is coming and when to expect it. Budgeting is easy because that income flow will continue as long as the employee keeps showing up for work.

Salespeople are often categorized as employees, but one key difference is that a portion of their income is tied to a commission. At one end of the spectrum are jobs like retail sales associates, who perform sales functions but are paid hourly. They might receive performance-based bonuses, but virtually all their income will come from a guaranteed hourly rate, which is the same way any other hourly employee would be paid.

On the other end of the sales spectrum are those who work on straight commission. This means that one hundred percent of the salesperson's income is derived from a commission. These types of roles, especially when the salesperson officially becomes as an independent contractor (insurance and real estate agents), bear little resemblance to the hourly rate compensation plan.

In these roles, it doesn't matter if the salesperson works ten hours a week or a hundred. That salesperson is only paid when there is a sale, usually a percentage of either the gross sales amount or the gross profit. There might be a delay in when the salesperson receives the money, such as a company policy where commission checks aren't cut until after the month or the quarter closes. Regardless of when the funds are received, the salesperson earns the commission when the sale takes place.

This type of compensation is very different than the hourly-based pay plan. Even if only ten or twenty percent of the total income is tied to a commission, if one salesperson sells more than another, that person will earn more money.

It also doesn't matter who worked more hours. In many cases, top performers work far less hours than the everybody else. They're able to do this because they have found ways to be more efficient.

This is the most significant difference between being paid for your time versus paid for results. A sales position that is tied to a commission will reward efficiency. When that commission represents a larger percentage of total income, the reward for efficiency will increase as well. Unfortunately, the opportunity to earn these bigger rewards also means the salesperson will assume more risk.

Someone who is paid hourly can forecast how much they will earn next week or next month. Someone in a straight commission role might anticipate a sale next month, but if that sale falls through there will be no income. Consider the example of a real estate agent who goes six months without a closing, but then has five in one month.

The point is that a commission-based pay plan will not provide the same steady amount of income that an hourly-based plan does. There will usually be peaks and valleys, so it is in the salesperson's best interest to stop planning and budgeting the same way as the hourly employee does.

Over time, the salesperson will establish and begin to anticipate an average amount of monthly income. It might be prudent for that salesperson to base personal spending budgets on an amount slightly lower than this average. Remember, it's an average, which means some months will be lower and some higher. If the monthly budget is based on a lower amount, it may not be necessary to dip into savings during the month's when the income is lower than average.

The biggest concern for any salesperson should be the months when income is significantly higher than average. Without question, those months should be celebrated, but the mistake most salespeople make is to start spending as if every month is going to be like that.

If the salesperson has had some kind of break through and the higher monthly amount will become the new average – Fantastic! Increase the monthly budget or go buy something. What those higher-than-average months usually mean though, is that the higher income is offsetting some lower-than-average months, which were either in the past or will come at some point in the future.

If they're in the past, that means the salesperson has experienced some lower-than-average months and likely has a pent-up desire to go live a little. Again, there is nothing wrong with celebrating a big month, but it would be in that salesperson's best interest to do it in moderation. This is especially true if the big month is offsetting some lower-than-average months that aren't even here yet.

There are two additional things to consider in our discussion about money.

- How do you view it?
- How do you use it?

Most of us were taught that money, by itself, is a bad thing. We've all heard things like, "money is the root of all evil," or "money can't buy happiness." When you consider that money is THE WAY to provide food, clothing and shelter for yourself and your family. It is THE WAY to provide dance lessons, sporting opportunities and further education for your children. It is THE WAY you'll be able to live comfortably when you're older or otherwise not able to work. If all this is true, then how can money be anything other than very good and very necessary?

Many of the things we believe about money have been subconsciously ingrained in us, and unfortunately most of the ones who did the ingraining weren't very good with money. Why not expand your knowledge base and study the habits of people who are good with money? If you were seeking relationship advice, would you rather talk to someone who has been married fifty years or someone down at the courthouse who just finalized their third divorce?

Intertwined and highly influenced by our perception of money are the choices we make in how we use money. If we subconsciously believe that money is evil, we're probably going to get rid of it as soon as we can. We'll go buy high ticket items and run up the credit card bills, but then one day we'll wake up and realize that broke, in debt and living paycheck-to-paycheck does not equate to happiness, contentment and a sense of fulfillment. This will be true no matter what your total gross income might be.

We'll look to those frugal savers who have money in the bank and a couple of passive income streams and wonder, "what do they know that I don't?" The good news is a lot of them will tell you if you just ask. In fact, some of them have even written down what they know in books. All that information is out there and available to you, but only if you seek it.

One for the money. Two for the show. Three to get ready. Now get out there and sell!

ABOUT THE AUTHOR

Charles Lewis has excelled at several sales and sales management positions across a range of industries including computer hardware, automobiles, and real estate.

He currently lives in Austin, Texas and produces YouTube videos to clarify and expand on many of the topics discussed in this book. He is available for speaking or training events and looks forward to helping you and your sales team achieve better results.

www.ingramcontent.com/pod-product-compliance
Lightning Source LLC
Chambersburg PA
CBHW070258220526
45465CB00004B/1647